LA RO(
TRAVEL (

Explore, Discover, And Indulge | Vibrant History, Beachside Bliss, And More!

Rita R. Nowlin

Copyright © Rita R. Nowlin 2023

All rights reserved. No part of this publication may be reproduced, distributed, or transmitted in any form or by any means, including photocopying, recording, or other electronic or mechanical methods, without the prior written permission of the publisher, except in the case of brief quotations embodied in critical reviews and certain other noncommercial uses permitted by copyright law.

Table Of Content

CHAPTER 1: AN OVERVIEW OF LA ROCHELLE. 9

Introduction To La Rochelle............... 9
La Rochelle's History........................ 12
Culture And Tradition....................... 14

CHAPTER 2. TRAVELLING TO LA ROCHELLE 17

Visa And Entry Requirements.......... 17
Currency And Budgeting................... 20
Travel Tips And Packing................... 22
How To Get There............................ 24
City-Wide Transportation.................. 25

CHAPTER 3: ACCOMMODATION SUGGESTIONS................................30

Hotels And Resorts.......................... 30
Bed And Breakfasts......................... 32
Vacation Rentals.............................. 34
Campgrounds And Hostels.............. 36
Information On Sightseeing Pass..... 38

CHAPTER 4: LA ROCHELLE ATTRACTIONS... 40

La Rochelle Aquarium......................40
Old Port (Vieux Port)........................ 42
Fort Boyard...................................... 44
La Rochelle Towers..........................46
Fortresses And Historical Sites........47
Historical Landmarks....................... 49
Museums & Art Galleries................. 50
Beaches And Outdoor Recreation... 52

3

CHAPTER 5: DINING AND CULINARY ARTS...54
  Charentais Cuisine Traditionnelle................ 54
  Seafood And Regional Delights...................... 55
  Cafes And Restaurants Suggestions............. 56
  A Dining Experience With A View................ 59
CHAPTER 6: SHOPPING IN LA ROCHELLE..... 62
  Souvenirs And Regional Products................ 62
  Markets And Shops... 64
  Shopping Avenues... 67
CHAPTER 7: ENTERTAINMENT AND NIGHTLIFE 70
  Pubs And Bars... 70
  Concerts And Live Music............................... 71
  Dancing And Nightclubs................................. 73
CHAPTER 8: LA ROCHELLE DAY TRIPS......... 76
  Île d'Oléron... 76
  Île de Ré.. 78
  Rochefort... 80
  Poitiers... 82
  Marais Poitevin (Green Venice)..................... 84
  Châtelaillon-Plage... 85
  Tours Of Cognac And Vineyards................... 87
CHAPTER 9: ITINERARIES SUGGESTIONS..... 90
  La Rochelle In One Day................................. 90
  Weekend Trip.. 92
  Activities For The Whole Family With Day Trip... 94
  Romantic Getaway.. 96
CHAPTER 10: USEFUL INFORMATION............ 98
  Weather Condition And Best Time To Visit..... 98

4

Etiquette And Customs...... 99
Communication And Language......101
Health And Safety Recommendations...... 102
Currency And Money Exchange...... 104
Money-Saving Tips...... 105
Basic French Phrases......107

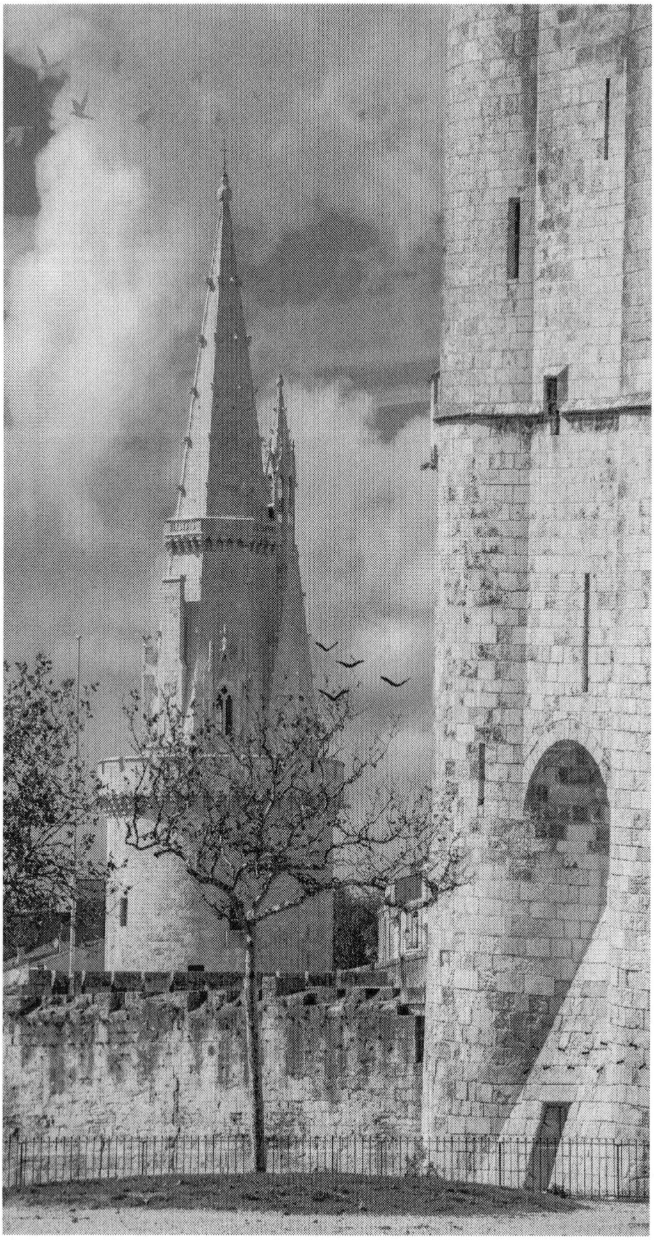

CHAPTER 1: AN OVERVIEW OF LA ROCHELLE

Introduction To La Rochelle

My voyage started in the busy Gare de La Rochelle, a train station that felt like a portal to another time. The exquisite Belle Époque building spoke of the travellers and adventurers who had passed through its doors. From there, I took a leisurely stroll through the cobblestone lanes of the Old Town, or "Vieux-Port," where history seemed to permeate from every stone.

The colourful façade of the waterfront buildings betrayed their secrets, having seen innumerable ships, traders, and explorers come and go.

The rhythmic clinking of sailboat masts against the backdrop of La Rochelle's renowned towers, Tour de la Lanterne and Tour de la Chaîne, formed a symphony of nautical tunes that reverberated through the salty sea wind. I was drawn to the quayside cafés, where I savoured fresh seafood while watching fishing boats return with their catch, a tribute to the city's lasting link to the sea.

I found La Rochelle's rich history and cultural gems as I ventured further into its centre. The magnificent Cathedral Saint-Louis loomed above the city, a tribute to the past's architectural magnificence. The nearby Musée nautical allowed me to dive into the region's intriguing nautical history, from the fabled expeditions of La Rochelle's seafarers to the commerce lines that once linked it to the rest of the globe.

I wandered down the shoreline as the sun set, watching the city lights glimmer and dance on the water's surface. La Rochelle's captivating combination of heritage and modernity made an unforgettable impression on my heart. It was a city that gently welcomed change while retaining its marine essence.

My trip to La Rochelle seemed like a journey back in time, a look into a world where the sea was more than just a background, but a way of life. The city's nautical mystery and rich history had captured me, leaving me wanting more as I prepared to discover its many hidden gems in the days ahead.

La Rochelle's History

The history of La Rochelle began in the 10th century, when it was a tiny fishing community. It increased in importance over the ages, becoming a busy port city vital to Europe's marine commerce routes. During the Hundred Years' War, the city's defensive walls, which still remain today, acted as a bulwark against English soldiers.

During the 17th century, one of La Rochelle's most defining occurrences happened. The city became a bastion for the Huguenots, who fought Cardinal Richelieu's authority and endured a protracted siege. The massive fortifications and the famed "Tour de la Lanterne," a lighthouse that acted as a jail for Huguenot leaders, bear witness to that turbulent time.

The scenic historic Port of La Rochelle, where historic sailing ships and contemporary yachts coexist, and the Maritime Museum, which highlights the city's nautical background, continue to carry on the city's maritime tradition.

The old streets of the city, ornamented with timber-framed buildings and cobblestone walks, create an environment that elegantly blends its past and present. La Rochelle is a living monument to its long past, an open book awaiting tourists from all over the world.

Culture And Tradition

La Rochelle's marine heritage is one of its most important cultural features. The Old Port, with its famous twin towers protecting the entrance, is a reminder of the town's maritime history. Walking down the quays, one may see historic fishing boats and sailboats, which symbolise the town's lasting link to the sea.

Traditions of La Rochelle are also commemorated through festivals and events. The Francofolies music festival and the Grand Pavois boat show are dynamic examples of the town's current cultural manifestations, bringing together inhabitants and visitors to enjoy music and nautical displays.

With wonderful seafood dishes and an abundance of fresh market goods, the local cuisine is another entryway to La Rochelle's traditions. Dining at a classic cafe or delighting on local oysters by the sea allows you to experience the region's unique flavours.

14

CHAPTER 2.
TRAVELLING TO LA ROCHELLE

Visa And Entry Requirements

France is a member of the Schengen Area, which implies that inhabitants of Schengen member nations can freely travel between them without a visa for up to 90 days during any 180-day period.

If you want a visa to enter France, you must apply at the French embassy or consulate in your native country. The visa requirements differ based on your nationality and the purpose of your trip, so make sure you verify the precise requirements for your scenario.

To enter France, you will need a valid passport in addition to a visa. Your passport must be valid for at least three months beyond your intended departure date from France.

If you want to stay in France for more than 90 days, you must apply for a long-stay visa. Students, labourers, and family members of French nationals are often granted long-stay visas.

Requirements for Admission: Visitors visiting France may be needed to produce proof of adequate cash for their stay, proof of lodging, and a return ticket, in addition to a valid passport.

Proof of Sufficient Funds: Visitors visiting France must be able to demonstrate that they have sufficient funds to maintain themselves throughout their stay. The amount of money necessary varies according to the duration of stay and the purpose of the visit. Tourists, for example, must have at least €61.50 per day, but business travellers must have at least €123.00 per day.

Proof of Accommodation: Visitors visiting France must be able to demonstrate that they have a place to stay while in the country. This can be accomplished by displaying a hotel reservation, a rental agreement, or a letter from a friend or family member verifying their stay with them.

Return Ticket : Visitors visiting France must be able to produce proof of a return ticket or the ability to exit the country at the end of their stay.

Additional Student and Worker Requirements: Students and employees who intend to stay in France for longer than 90 days must get a long-stay visa. Long-term visas need the submission of extra papers, such as proof of attendance in a school or university or proof of employment.

Currency And Budgeting

France's currency is the euro (€). Banks, currency exchange offices, and certain hotels accept Euros for exchange. It is best to convert some money before you leave, as airport exchange rates might be less favourable.

Budgeting in La Rochelle:
- **lodging**: From affordable hostels to luxury hotels, La Rochelle provides a wide range of lodging alternatives to suit all budgets. Consider staying in a hostel or guesthouse if you are on a low budget.

Alternatively, there are self-catering flats and homes for rent.
- **Food**: Dining out in La Rochelle might be costly, but there are methods to cut costs. Look for restaurants that have fixed menus or prix fixe meals. You may also save money by dining during lunch, when many eateries offer cheaper menus. If you're on a limited budget, try preparing your own meals in your lodging.
- **Activities**: There are many free or low-cost activities in La Rochelle, such as visiting the Old Town, the beach, and the parks. Many museums and art galleries also provide free entry on certain days of the week. If you want to do a lot of touring, consider getting a La Rochelle City Pass, which provides free entrance to several of the city's best attractions.

- **Transportation**: La Rochelle has an excellent public transit system, making it simple to travel around without a car. For public transit, you may buy a day pass or a weekly pass. If you intend to hire a car, remember to add in the cost of parking and petrol.

Travel Tips And Packing

- **Weather-appropriate Clothing**: Because La Rochelle has a temperate marine environment, bring clothing that may be worn in a variety of conditions. Lightweight layers, a rain jacket, and sturdy walking shoes are required.
- **Sun Protection**: With so many bright days ahead, don't forget to bring sunscreen, sunglasses, and a wide-brimmed hat to protect yourself from the sun.

- Type E plugs are used in French power sockets. Bring the necessary adapters and chargers for your electronic gadgets.
- While many people speak English, knowing a few simple French words may enhance your experience and demonstrate respect for the local culture.
- **Travel Documents**: Before leaving, make sure you have a valid passport, travel insurance, and any necessary visas.
- Carry some euros with you for modest transactions, however credit cards are usually accepted.
- **A tourist map or guidebook** will assist you in navigating the town and discovering its various attractions.
- Pack swimsuits, beach towels, and a nice book if you intend to enjoy the lovely beaches.

- **Camera and charges**: The lovely streets and ancient landmarks of La Rochelle provide excellent photo opportunities, so bring your camera and any required charges.

How To Get There

The train is one of the most frequent ways to get to La Rochelle. The town has a well-connected train station, which allows it to be reached from major French cities such as Paris and Bordeaux. The TGV (high-speed rail) network provides a quick and picturesque ride to La Rochelle, enabling you to take in the stunning French scenery along the route.

If you prefer to fly, La Rochelle has its own international airport, La Rochelle-Île de Ré Airport. Direct flights from several European cities are available, making it a handy alternative for foreign travellers.

La Rochelle is conveniently accessible by vehicle for people who prefer road trips. The town is well connected to the French highway system, giving it a convenient and adaptable option for visitors.

City-Wide Transportation

Bus: A single Ticket is €1.50, while a day pass is €5.00. A weekly pass is also available for €15.00. Tickets are available for purchase on the bus or at vending machines stationed at bus stops.

Boats: You may use a boat to go around La Rochelle if you want to see more of the scenery. A variety of boat companies provide excursions and cruises of the harbour and surrounding

23

region. Prices vary based on the duration and style of cruise, but a basic one-hour excursion should cost approximately €10.00.

Bicycles: La Rochelle is a bike-friendly city with a plethora of bicycle rental options. There are also various bike trails around the city that make it simple to get around on two wheels. Bicycle rental costs differ based on the type of bike rented and the duration of time rented. A day rental, on the other hand, will cost roughly €10.00.

Other Modes of Transportation: In addition to public transit, La Rochelle has a few more modes of mobility. Taxis, ride-sharing applications, and automobile rentals are examples of these.

- **Taxis** are more expensive than public transit, but they are more handy and widely available. Ride-hailing applications like Uber and Lyft are also accessible in La Rochelle, and they are a less expensive alternative to taxis.

- **Car rentals** are the most expensive mode of transportation, but they provide the greatest flexibility. If you want to do a lot of sightseeing outside of the city centre, renting a car may be an excellent alternative.

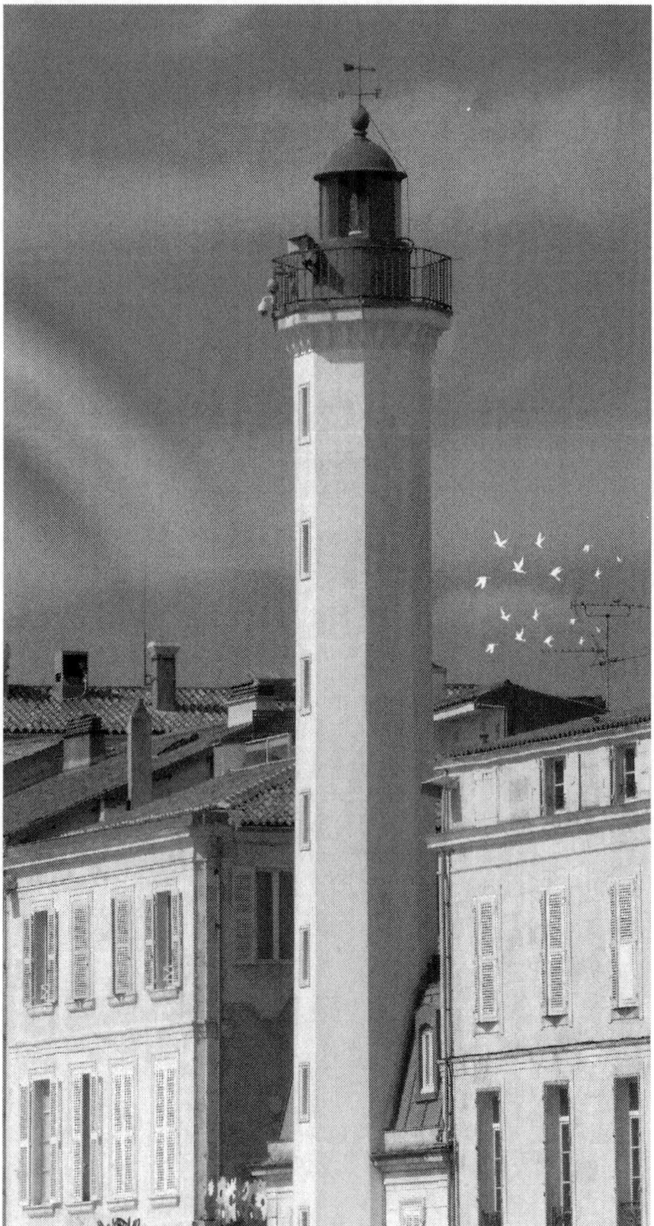

CHAPTER 3: ACCOMMODATION SUGGESTIONS

Hotels And Resorts

Budget:

- **ibis La Rochelle Centre Historique**: This low-cost hotel is in the heart of the historic district, near to all of the city's major attractions. Rooms begin around €60 per night.
- **ibis La Rochelle Vieux-Port**: Located in the historic port, this hotel offers spectacular views of the harbour. Rooms begin around €70 per night.
- **hotelF1 La Rochelle Angoulins**: This little hotel is located just outside of La Rochelle, although it is still easily

accessible to the city centre. Rooms begin around €20 per night.

Mid-Range:

- **Hôtel Les Brises:** Located in the historic harbour, this hotel has a rooftop terrace with panoramic views of the city. Rooms begin about €100 per night.
- **Hôtel du Centre:** This magnificent ancient structure is located in the heart of the historic centre. Rooms begin about €120 per night.
- **Hôtel Saint Nicolas:** Located in the historic harbour, this hotel has a direct view of the towers. Rooms begin about €130 per night.

Luxury:

- **Hôtel & Spa du Château:** This luxurious hotel is located just outside of La Rochelle in a 17th-century castle. It has a spa, a pool, and a golf course. Rooms begin around €200 per night.

- **Maison des Ambassadeurs**: A boutique hotel in the heart of the historic district. It offers a spa, a swimming pool, and a patio with city views. Rooms begin around €250 per night.
- **Yelloh! Village Les Atlantides:** This resort is located on the outskirts of La Rochelle and has immediate beach access. It contains a swimming pool, water slides, and a range of other family-friendly activities. A mobile house starts at roughly €150 per night.

Bed And Breakfasts

- **Escale Rochelaise:** Located in the centre of La Rochelle's old town, only steps from the harbour and the market, this exquisite bed and breakfast is a must-see.

It has four tastefully fitted bedrooms with a sauna and hot tub for visitors to use. Prices for a double room start at €150 per night.

- **La Belle Amarre**: This delightful bed and breakfast is set in a quiet residential area near the beach. It has four big bedrooms, a patio, and a garden where visitors may rest. Prices for a double room start at €120 per night.

- **Terre en Vue** is a bed & breakfast in a peaceful neighbourhood just outside of town. It has three comfortable bedrooms, a wide yard, and a great breakfast in the dining room. The nightly rate begins at €80.

- **Chambres d'hôtes Le Clos Bleu**: This tiny bed and breakfast is located in a quiet residential neighbourhood, just a short walk from the city centre. It has two elegantly appointed bedrooms as well as a separate garden where visitors may unwind. Prices for a double room start at €100 per night.

- **Chambres d'hôtes Les Minimes**: Located in the Minimes neighbourhood, this family-run bed & breakfast is just a short walk from the beach and the harbour. It has three pleasant bedrooms, a communal kitchen, and a living area. Prices for a double room start at €80 per night.

Vacation Rentals

- **L'Art Studio hyper centre**: This one-bedroom apartment is located in the centre of La Rochelle, only steps away from the Old Port and the town hall. It has been recently remodelled and provides everything you need for a comfortable stay, including a fully supplied kitchen, a washer and dryer, and a private balcony. The cost each night is €100.

- **Nid douillet T2 wifi centre historique 3 étoiles**: This two-bedroom apartment is likewise located in the Old Port neighbourhood, near to all of the shops, restaurants and attractions. It offers a fireplace in the living area, a fully supplied kitchen, and a private balcony. The cost each night is €120.

- **Appart Christelle**: This two-bedroom apartment is in a quiet residential area, just a short walk from the beach. It offers a large living area with a sofa bed, a full kitchen, and a private patio. The cost per night is €130.

- **Villa Les Palmiers**: This four-bedroom property is in a gated neighbourhood not far from La Rochelle. It comes with a private pool, a huge yard, and a fully fitted kitchen. The cost each night is €250.

- **Maison de ville avec jardin**: This four-bedroom townhouse with a garden is located in the centre of La Rochelle, only minutes from the ocean and the Old Port. It offers a private garden as well as a fully fitted kitchen and a washer and dryer. The cost each night is €300.

Campgrounds And Hostels

Campgrounds:

- **Camping Municipal de l'Atlantique**: Located just a short walk from the beach, this campground provides a range of amenities such as a swimming pool, playground, and restaurant. Tent sites start at €15 per night while caravan pitches start at €25 per night.

- **Camping des Deux Plages**: Located on a peninsula between two beaches, this campground provides breathtaking views of the ocean. Tent sites start at €18 per night while caravan pitches start at €28 per night.
- **Camping La Rochelle Sud**: Located just outside of the city centre, this campground provides a more relaxing ambiance. Tent sites start at €12 per night while caravan pitches start at €20 per night.

Hostels:
- **Hostel La Rochelle**: Located in the middle of the city, this hostel provides a selection of dorm and private rooms. Prices for a dorm bed start at €19 per night and go up to €35 per night for a private room.

- **People Hostel La Rochelle**: Located in a historic building in the city centre, this hostel provides a mix of dorm and private rooms. Prices for a dorm bed start at €18 per night and go up to €32 per night for a private room.
- **City Hostel La Rochelle**: Located in a calm section of the city centre, this hostel provides a selection of dorm and private rooms. Prices for a dorm bed start at €17 per night and go up to €30 per night for a private room.

Information On Sightseeing Pass

The La Rochelle Océan Pass comes in three different lengths: 48 hours (€44), 72 hours (€57), and 7 days (€75). The Aquarium La Rochelle, the Towers of La Rochelle, the Maritime Museum, and the Île de Ré are all included in the Pass. It also covers unlimited public transit use.

La Rochelle city pass: This card provides free access to La Rochelle's two most popular attractions, the Aquarium La Rochelle and the Towers of La Rochelle. It also includes a free harbour boat trip and unlimited public transit. The City Pass La Rochelle comes in two lengths: 24 hours (€28) and 48 hours (€38).

Which sightseeing pass is best for you is determined on your interests and length of stay in La Rochelle. The La Rochelle City Pass is a wonderful alternative if you only intend on visiting the city for a day or two. If you intend to stay longer and explore sites in the surrounding region, the La Rochelle Océan Pass is a better option.

CHAPTER 4: LA ROCHELLE ATTRACTIONS

La Rochelle Aquarium

This incredible aquatic refuge, hidden on the coast of the Bay of Biscay, provides an enthralling adventure for tourists of all ages.

The aquarium has a remarkable collection of over 12,000 marine animals from the depths of the Atlantic Ocean, displaying a diverse range of species in elegantly designed and instructive exhibits. As you go through the dimly lit corridors, you'll come face to face with beautiful jellyfish, colourful corals, and huge sharks, all of which are gently traversing their watery surroundings.

One of the most impressive attractions is the gigantic 1.5 million-liter tank, which houses a beautiful reproduction of the Charente-Maritime seafloor. Visitors are enchanted as schools of fish, exquisite rays, and even a friendly loggerhead sea turtle pass past. The aquarium's dedication to conservation and education is clear throughout, with compelling lectures and interactive displays highlighting the critical need of conserving our seas.

Old Port (Vieux Port)

The Old Port of La Rochelle is a historic treasure where the past and contemporary coexist together.

The well-preserved mediaeval architecture, with its timber-framed homes and stone towers, will enchant you as you meander down the cobblestone streets. The three distinctive mediaeval towers, which include the majestic Tour de la Chaîne and Tour Saint-Nicolas, stand proudly at the harbor's entrance, reminding tourists of the city's nautical legacy.

The Old Port is a hive of activity, with small cafes, seafood eateries, and artisan stores. It's the ideal spot for fresh seafood, a relaxing café au lait, or shopping for local goods. Fishermen go about their daily activities near the water's side, affording a look into the traditional way of life that still exists in La Rochelle.

The Maritime Museum, situated in the ancient naval barracks, is a must-see for history buffs, providing an insightful peek into the region's maritime heritage. You may also take a boat excursion to see surrounding islands like Île de Ré and Île d'Aix, adding a marine adventure to your vacation.

The Old Port comes alive in the evening with street performers, live music, and a lively atmosphere.

Fort Boyard

This magnificent citadel, located off the coast of La Rochelle in the scenic Charente-Maritime region of France, is an iconic emblem of the region. Its origins extend back to the early nineteenth century, and it has performed a variety of functions throughout its history, ranging from military stronghold to film set for the popular TV game show.

Visiting Fort Boyard is a thrilling experience in and of itself. Only by boat can you reach the stronghold in the middle of the sea. The sheer size and towering construction of the fort will take your breath away as you approach. It is a remarkable architectural masterpiece because to its distinctive circular form, enormous stone walls, and harsh look.

Exploring the fort reveals a rich history. You may walk through the dimly lighted rooms where soldiers used to live and work, feeling the weight of history in every stone. It now functions as a museum, providing insight into the life and purpose of this mysterious edifice.

Furthermore, Fort Boyard is surrounded by the spectacular natural splendour of the Atlantic Ocean, making it an ideal setting for breathtaking photographs.

La Rochelle Towers

The Tour Saint-Nicolas, Tour de la Chaîne, and Tour de la Lanterne are magnificent mediaeval fortifications that have defended the town's harbour for centuries. When you enter these old structures, you'll be taken back to a time when La Rochelle was a thriving centre for trade and nautical activity.

Climbing the narrow stone steps to the pinnacle of these towers provides stunning views over the Atlantic Ocean and the picturesque old town. The Tour de la Lanterne, in particular, is famous for its magnificent 15th-century lantern, which formerly directed mariners home.

Aside from its architectural beauty and historic value, these towers serve as a living history book of La Rochelle. The displays and exhibits within the towers provide visitors with a better knowledge of the town's maritime history, importance in trade and commerce, and the obstacles it encountered throughout the years.

Fortresses And Historical Sites

The La Rochelle Towers, which historically functioned as a powerful defence against invaders and pirates, are one of the city's most recognisable sights. The Tour de la Lanterne, with its unique lantern chamber, is a work of mediaeval art. Nearby, the massive Tour de la Chaîne, named after the chain used to seal the city's harbour each night, stands as a tribute to the city's nautical power.

The old part of the city is a maze of small cobblestone alleyways surrounded by timber-framed homes that have seen centuries of history. The Old Port, with its colourful quayside eateries, has a timeless appeal that makes it ideal for leisurely strolls and people-watching.

For a deeper dig into history, go to the Musée du Nouveau Monde, which highlights La Rochelle's links to the New World, or the Musée Maritime, which explores the town's naval background. Fort Boyard, the enigmatic bastion in the middle of the sea, is a short drive away and makes for an exciting day excursion.

Historical Landmarks

Begin your journey in the renowned La Rochelle Old Port, Saint-Nicolas Tower, which guards the entrance to the Old Port, serves as a sentinel of La Rochelle's nautical past. It was built in the 14th century and portrays stories of mediaeval times, naval wars, and the city's resistance against sieges. Climb the towers for panoramic views of the Atlantic Ocean and the bustling harbour below

The Tour de la Chaîne, a mediaeval tower turned museum, is a reminder of the city's maritime heritage. Its mediaeval design, replete with a hefty chain used to collect tolls from passing ships, reflects the prosperity of La Rochelle during its commercial heydays.

La Rochelle's significance in the Protestant Reformation is commemorated at the Huguenot Heritage. This city was a haven for Huguenots, and the Museum of Protestant History honours their hardships and victories, providing insights into a critical moment in French history.

Explore the Museum of the New World for a more moving experience, which explains the tale of La Rochelle's role in the transatlantic slave trade and its influence on the Americas.

Museums & Art Galleries

The **Musée du Nouveau Monde**, or **Museum of the New World,** is a must-see institution that highlights the city's major role in the period of discovery, notably during expeditions to the Americas. It is home to a large collection of artefacts, including Native American and colonial antiquities, as well as significant historical displays.

The **Musée des Beaux-Arts (Fine Arts Museum)** is a treasure trove of European paintings, sculptures, and decorative arts spanning centuries for art enthusiasts. The varied collection of the museum includes works by prominent painters such as Delacroix, Sisley, and Chardin.

The main centre of La Rochelle is peppered with art galleries featuring modern and local artists, providing a look into the city's thriving creative environment. Strolling around these galleries is a fantastic chance to admire the region's modern art and workmanship.

Beaches And Outdoor Recreation

With its golden sands and clean seas, **Plage de la Concurrence** is ideal for sunbathing and swimming. It's a terrific place for families with beautiful views of the old La Rochelle harbour.

Plage des Minimes is the place to be for those looking for more adventure. Water sports enthusiasts are invited to try their hand at windsurfing, kite surfing, or sailing on its long stretch of sandy beach. The active beachside promenade is dotted with restaurants, cafes, and stores and serves as a buzzing centre of activity.

Nature enthusiasts may visit the adjacent Île de Ré, which has unspoilt scenery and lovely settlements and is accessible via bridge. Cycling on the island's designated routes is a popular way to enjoy the surroundings.

Aside from beaches, La Rochelle's coastal location offers several of options for fishing, boating, and even dolphin-watching trips. The gorgeous coastal routes, which provide amazing views of the Atlantic Ocean, are ideal for hikers and bikers.

CHAPTER 5: DINING AND CULINARY ARTS

Charentais Cuisine Traditionnelle

A gourmet excursion in La Rochelle would be incomplete without sampling the region's famed seafood. Freshly obtained Atlantic Ocean oysters, mussels, and fish are vital components of Charentais cuisine. The renowned **'Mouclade**,' a creamy mussel dish laced with saffron and Cognac, demonstrates the region's seafood skill.

The Charentais are especially proud of their local cheeses, like as the well-known **Chabichou**, a creamy goat's cheese that goes perfectly with crusty bread. The famed **'Beurre Blanc**,' a rich butter sauce, is an iconic complement to fish, demonstrating the region's culinary skill.

While at La Rochelle, don't pass up the chance to try **'Pineau des Charentes**,' a wonderful fortified wine that pairs perfectly with the local food. The vibrant markets of the city provide a true flavour of Charentais Cuisine Traditionnelle, with fresh fruits, vegetables, and artisanal items awaiting discovery.

Seafood And Regional Delights

- **Huîtres Marennes-Oléron (Marennes-Oléron oysters):** These famous French oysters are cultivated in the Marennes-Oléron bay, right off the coast of La Rochelle.

- **Pintade au Pineau**: This meal is created with guinea fowl that has been marinated and cooked in Pineau, a sweet fortified wine from the Cognac area.

- **Gâteau Nantais (Nantes cake):** Made with almonds, sugar, and butter, this rich and delectable cake is commonly served with rum or crème fraîche.

- **Cagouilles**: a regional speciality of succulent snails served in a delicious garlic and parsley sauce.

Cafes And Restaurants Suggestions

Cafes

- **Le Garden Café:** Located in the heart of La Rochelle's historic city centre, this cosy café serves a variety of coffees, teas, pastries, and light meals. The outside patio is ideal for people-watching and taking in the ambience of the city.

- **Le Café Molière:** This well-known establishment is noted for its superb coffee and pleasant service. It's also a terrific spot for a full French breakfast, complete with croissants, pain au chocolat, and fresh fruit juice.

- **Nagoya K'fée:** This Japanese-inspired café provides a one-of-a-kind coffee experience. The coffee beans are roasted on-site, and the baristas are true professionals. Nagoya K'fée also serves Japanese snacks and pastries.

Restaurants

- **Le Café du Nord:** This typical French café on the riverside provides breathtaking views of the harbour. The menu includes typical French cuisine such as moules frites, steak frites, and coq au vin.

- **Christopher Coutanceau:** This Michelin-starred restaurant serves a sophisticated French tasting menu. The meals are tastefully presented and prepared using only the freshest local ingredients.

- **Saint Nicolas**: This beautiful restaurant in a former church gives a one-of-a-kind dining experience. The menu includes a range of unique seafood dishes as well as classic French cuisine.
- **La Yole de Chris:** This well-known restaurant is noted for its fresh fish and creative meals. The menu changes seasonally to reflect the day's freshest fish.
- **Chez Victor:** For almost 50 years, this family-run restaurant has served classic French food. The menu includes classic meals such as boeuf bourguignon and confit de canard.

A Dining Experience With A View

Restaurant Les Flots, a Michelin-starred restaurant in the centre of the Old Port, is one of the most popular alternatives. The dining area of the restaurant has floor-to-ceiling windows with magnificent views of the harbour, the three distinctive towers, and the Atlantic Ocean beyond. The menu emphasises inventive seafood dishes prepared with the finest local ingredients.

Restaurant Gaée, located on the Quai Louis Prunier, immediately opposite the Vieux Port, is another wonderful choice. The patio of the restaurant provides amazing views of the harbour and the city skyline. The menu includes classic French cuisine as well as more innovative interpretations.

Consider **Le Belvédère**, which is located on the top floor of the Musée Maritime de La Rochelle, for a more relaxed eating experience. The restaurant has sweeping views of the city, the harbour, and the neighbouring islands. The menu includes a mix of French and foreign meals, as well as local seafood delicacies.

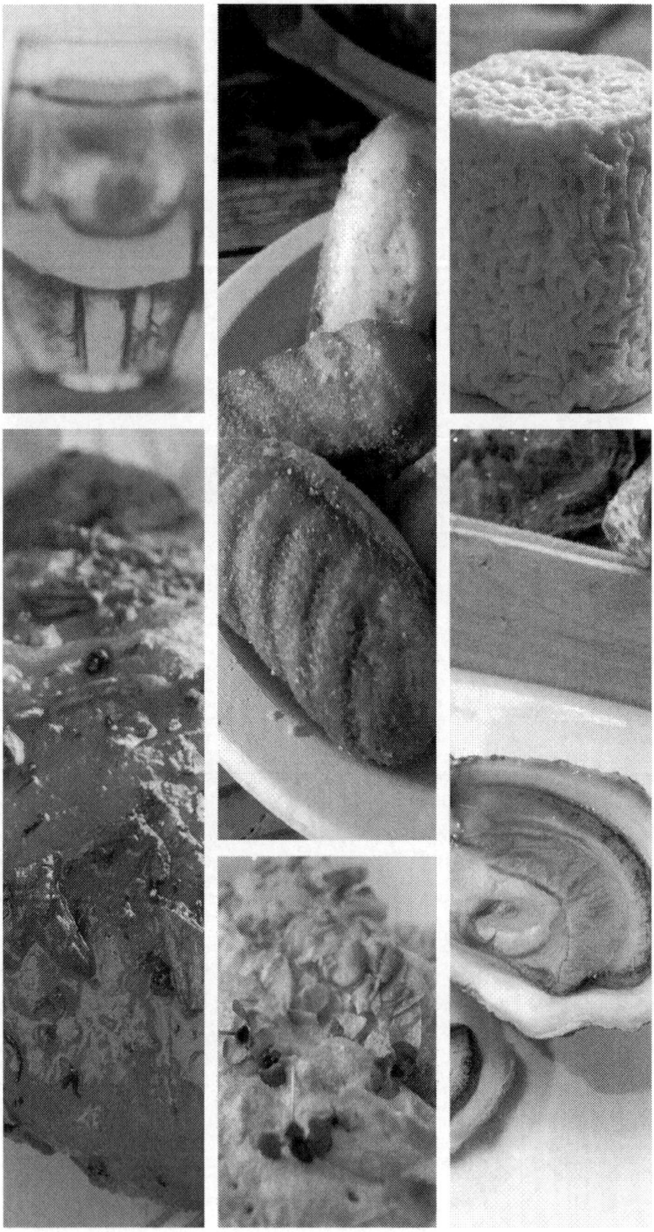

CHAPTER 6: SHOPPING IN LA ROCHELLE

Souvenirs And Regional Products

As you meander through its cobblestone streets and waterfront, you'll meet a broad selection of souvenirs and regional items that represent the town's unique character.

One of the most popular souvenirs is, naturally, nautical-themed. From tiny sailboats and lighthouses to seashell jewelry, these things not only make for wonderful souvenirs but also serve as memories of La Rochelle's marine history. The locally produced, bright wooden buoys are another favourite choice, signifying the town's strong marine culture.

For those with a flair for gastronomic experiences, La Rochelle provides a wonderful assortment of regional goods. Indulge in the tastes of the sea with freshly caught seafood, including luscious oysters and mussels. Don't forget to pick up a bottle of Charente-Maritime's renowned Pineau des Charentes, a wonderful combination of grape juice and Cognac, or some Cognac itself, a celebrated local liquor.

If you're interested in knowing more about La Rochelle and its history, you may acquire a selection of books and maps at the city's bookstores and tourist office

Markets And Shops

Markets

One of the greatest locations to enjoy La Rochelle's local culture and food is at one of its many markets. The largest and most popular market is the **Marché Central**, which is held everyday in the city center. The market is set in a lovely 19th-century structure and contains a large range of vendors selling fresh vegetables, fish, pork, cheese, bread, and other local delicacies.

On Wednesdays and Saturdays, the Marché Central widens to cover the adjacent streets, where visitors may find a range of non-food things, such as apparel, accessories, and souvenirs.

Another popular market is the **Marché de La Pallice**, which is held every Sunday morning in the La Pallice district. This market is smaller than the Marché Central, but it has a more casual atmosphere and has a variety of vendors offering fresh vegetables, seafood, and other local items.

In addition to these two big markets, La Rochelle also boasts a variety of smaller markets that are hosted throughout the week. These markets are often smaller and more specialized, but they may be a terrific location to discover unusual presents and souvenirs.

Shops

In addition to the food markets, La Rochelle features a variety of boutique boutiques along its cobblestone lanes. Whether you're seeking for clothes, souvenirs, or antiques, the city's charming shops provide a choice of things. The narrow streets of the ancient city center are home to lovely, family-owned stores selling anything from trendy French apparel to unique handicrafts.

La Rochelle also features a range of stores where guests may purchase anything from apparel and accessories to home items and gifts. The major shopping district is the Vieux Port (Old Port), which is characterised with tiny lanes and lovely stores.

In the Vieux Port, travellers may discover a variety of businesses providing apparel, accessories, and jewelry. There are also a lot of businesses offering souvenirs, such as postcards, t-shirts, and caps.

Another famous shopping district is the Rue Saint-Nicolas, which is a pedestrianized street dotted with stores and restaurants. In the Rue Saint-Nicolas, tourists may discover a range of stores providing apparel, accessories, household items, and souvenirs.

In addition to these two main retail centres, La Rochelle also boasts a variety of additional stores distributed across the city. These businesses often sell more specialized things, such as antiques, literature, and art

Shopping Avenues

The major retail street of La Rochelle is **Rue du Palais**. It is bordered with a variety of boutiques, including clothes, shoe, and souvenir stores. Rue du Palais also has a variety of restaurants and cafés, making it a wonderful area to take a breather while shopping.

Rue du Port: This street runs along the shore and houses a variety of restaurants, cafés, and stores. Rue du Port sells anything from apparel and souvenirs to nautical gear.

Rue du Marché: Located in the city centre, this street is home to a variety of stores providing fresh fruit, seafood, and other local items. It also houses the Marché du Centre Ville, La Rochelle's largest and most popular market.

Rue de la Grosse Horloge: The renowned Grosse Horloge, a 15th-century clock tower, is located on this route. The street is also lined with a variety of boutiques, including clothes, shoe, and souvenir shops.

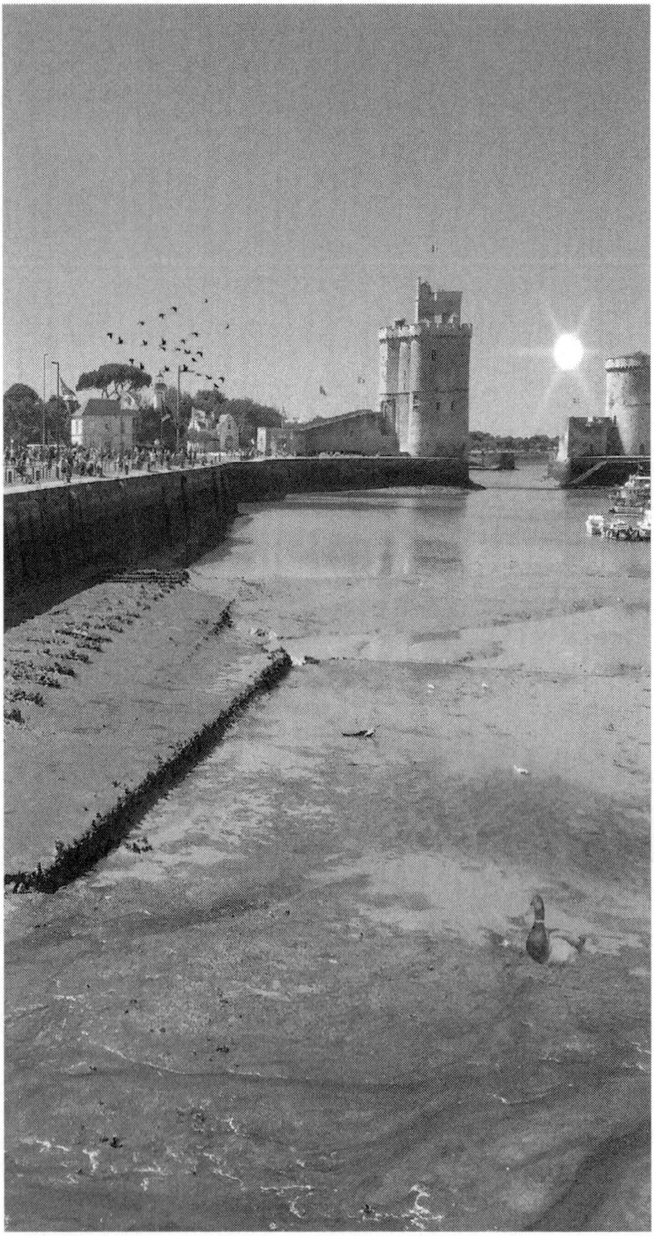

CHAPTER 7: ENTERTAINMENT AND NIGHTLIFE

Pubs And Bars

- **The Famous pub**: This unassuming tavern is ideal for a pint of beer and some traditional pub fare. In addition to a great assortment of cocktails and other drinks, The Famous Pub features a cheerful and welcoming ambiance.
- **Mac Ewan's pub**: This Scottish tavern is popular with both visitors and locals. Mac Ewan's Pub serves a broad variety of beers and whiskies, as well as traditional Scottish meals and live music on select weeknights.
- **The General Humbert's:** This Irish bar is ideal for a Guinness and some live

Irish music. The General Humbert's also boasts a cheerful and welcoming ambiance, making it an excellent location for meeting new people and establishing new friends.

- **Le Casier**: A contemporary cocktail bar where you may have a well-crafted martini or two. Le Casier also boasts a trendy and casual environment, making it an excellent choice for beginning or ending your evening in La Rochelle.
- **Le Mayflower**: This bustling music establishment is ideal for seeing a live band or DJ play. Le Mayflower also provides a huge assortment of beverages as well as a large dance floor.

Concerts And Live Music

The numerous music venues in the city appeal to a wide range of preferences. You may be swaying to the strains of traditional French chansons in an intimate café or rocking to the beats of current rock at a local hotspot. The bustling Old Port is one of the highlights, as street musicians frequently create an impromptu concert scene that is both enthralling and comforting.

Consider attending a concert at La Coursive, a renowned cultural centre that organises a range of events, including classical music, jazz, and world music, for a more formal experience. Open-air activities such as Les Francofolies, a well-known music festival, enchant La Rochelle with the sounds of top singers from France and abroad during the summer.

Whatever your musical tastes, La Rochelle's live music scene provides a remarkable and stimulating experience that will surely improve your visit to this beautiful city on the Atlantic coast.

Dancing And Nightclubs

The vibrant Old Port district is the epicentre of La Rochelle's nightlife. You'll find a wide range of nightclubs catering to various tastes, from techno to salsa and everything in between. The cadence of DJ-spun sounds, live bands, and even the rare international guest artist fills the dance floors.

La Sirène, a music hall and nightclub wrapped into one, is one of La Rochelle's notable venues. It is well-known for presenting varied music events and is a popular place to dance. Le P'tit Bar offers a cosy environment with a sophisticated cocktail menu, suited for a more refined night out, for those looking for a more private and upmarket experience.

However, La Rochelle's nightlife is not limited to the Old Port. The city's numerous pubs and clubs are dispersed across the city, ensuring that you can locate the ideal location to dance the night away.

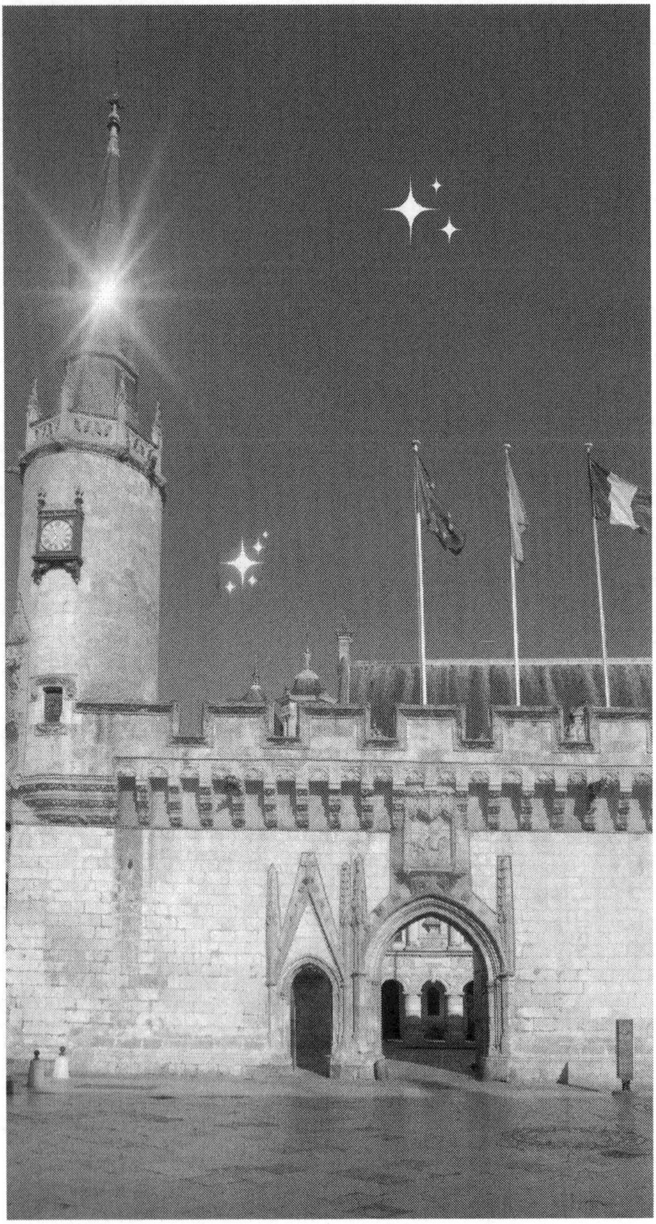

CHAPTER 8: LA ROCHELLE DAY TRIPS

Île d'Oléron

The largest island in the Charente-Maritime region, Île d'Oléron, provides a unique combination of natural beauty, historic attractions, and coastal charm.

Begin your tour by passing across the spectacular bridge that connects the mainland to the island. Take in the breathtaking scenery of

Île d'Oléron, from pristine beaches to lush woods. Visit Château d'Oléron, a charming hamlet with a bustling oyster market and the spectacular Citadel, a mediaeval stronghold with panoramic views of the surrounding countryside.

Visit the majestic Fort Boyard, which has been on television shows, and explore the quaint fishing towns like Saint-Denis-d'Oléron, where colourful boats bob in the harbour, for a sense of the island's rich nautical heritage.

Don't pass on the island's culinary delights. In one of the numerous coastal restaurants, savour fresh seafood, notably the famed oysters. And don't forget to treat yourself to some handcrafted ice cream from a local parlour.

Île de Ré

Île de Ré is easily accessible from La Rochelle through a beautiful bridge, making it an ideal day trip destination.

As you cross the bridge, you'll be met with the tranquil mood of the island, which is defined by small villages, gorgeous beaches, and idyllic scenery. The lovely architecture of the island, with its white-washed buildings embellished with colourful shutters and brilliant hollyhocks, provides a postcard-perfect backdrop for your explore.

On Île de Ré, cycling is the preferred means of transportation, with an extensive network of bike lanes winding through salt marshes and along the shore. Rent a bicycle and ride about the island at your leisure, stopping at small markets to sample fresh seafood, oysters, and regional wines.

The island also has beautiful beaches where you may rest, swim, or participate in water sports. Visit the UNESCO World Heritage site of Saint-Martin-de-Ré, with its old walls and picturesque harbour. As the day comes to an end, take a minute to view the beautiful sunset over the sea before returning to La Rochelle.

Rochefort

Rochefort, just a short drive or train trip away, provides a fascinating voyage through time as well as a taste of maritime tradition.

Begin the day by visiting the Corderie Royale, a massive 17th-century rope-making plant that once supplied the French navy. The majestic stone structure, surrounded by lovely gardens, is now a museum showcasing France's naval history. The Hermione, a beautifully rebuilt 18th-century frigate that played an important part in the American Revolutionary War, sits nearby.

After learning about maritime history, meander around the picturesque alleys of Rochefort. Admire the town's exquisite architecture, explore the local markets, and dine on classic French cuisine at the town's cafés and restaurants.

Don't pass up the opportunity to unwind at the Thermes de Rochefort, a historic thermal bathhouse famous for its medicinal waters. This is the place to decompress if you're seeking for relaxation or rejuvenation.

Poitiers

Poitiers, only a few hours distant by rail or vehicle, with a distinct combination of mediaeval and contemporary elements.

Begin your day in Poitiers by touring the city's mediaeval centre, which is surrounded with tiny cobblestone lanes adorned with half-timbered buildings and antique churches. The majestic Notre-Dame la Grande, noted for its elaborate sculptures and lovely exterior, is a must-see. The Palace of Poitiers, a historical jewel that previously functioned as a royal home, lies nearby.

Foodies will like the local food. Poitiers has a variety of typical French bistros and patisseries where you may indulge in regional specialities such as the famed Poitou goat cheese. After lunch, visit the Futuroscope theme park, a one-of-a-kind destination that specialises in cutting-edge multimedia and cinematic experiences.

To round up your day, take a stroll along the Clain River and possibly visit the Jardin des Plantes, a beautiful botanical park.

Marais Poitevin (Green Venice)

This unique wetland region is a tranquil and attractive place within a short drive from La Rochelle.

The trip to Marais Poitevin begins with a lovely drive through picturesque French countryside. As you reach the marshes, the environment changes into a stunning network of canals, lush foliage, and charming towns. You may float along the quiet canals on a classic flat-bottomed boat, surrounded by a tapestry of aquatic flora and creatures. The boat journey provides an enthralling insight into the area's diverse wildlife, which includes herons, kingfishers, and other waterfowl.

While exploring the marshland's colourful settlements, you may stop at waterside cafés to sample local food. Freshwater fish recipes and regional delicacies are popular in Marais Poitevin. You may meander through the scenic alleys of Coulon and explore tiny art galleries, craft stores, and local markets.

Châtelaillon-Plage

Châtelaillon-Plage, just a short drive from La Rochelle, is a picturesque coastal town famed for its stunning beaches and lively atmosphere.

When you arrive at Châtelaillon-Plage, you will be met with a gorgeous promenade that runs down the coast and is adorned with colourful beachfront residences, cafés, and stores. The beach itself, with its smooth golden sands and enticing seas, is the major draw. Châtelaillon-Plage provides something for everyone, whether you want to relax in the sun, go for a leisurely swim, or participate in water sports.

While strolling around town, you'll come across a charming market area where open-air eateries serve fresh seafood, regional cuisines, and local wines. For those looking for leisure and enjoyment, Châtelaillon-Plage also has a stunning casino and a thalassotherapy spa.

A visit to the 19th-century Châtelaillon-Plage Train Station, with its lovely architecture, is a must for history buffs. Moreover, the town holds a variety of events and festivals throughout the year, so be sure to check the local calendar for any interesting activities taking place during your stay.

Tours Of Cognac And Vineyards

This voyage through the Charente area offers visitors to discover the quaint town of Cognac and its lush vineyards, all within a day's drive of the seaside beauty of La Rochelle.

The day begins with a lovely drive through vineyards that reach as far as the eye can see. Visitors may enjoy guided tours of local wineries and sample excellent blends while learning about the traditional Cognac manufacturing process. For anyone looking to savour the rich history and flavour of this French spirit, a visit to one of the prominent Cognac houses, such as Hennessy or Rémy Martin, is a must.

The tour then continues to Cognac, where cobblestone streets and old buildings await you. A visit to the Château Royal de Cognac, a 10th-century fortress, gives insight into the town's mediaeval heritage. Lunch at a small café allows you to sample regional food matched with superb Cognac.

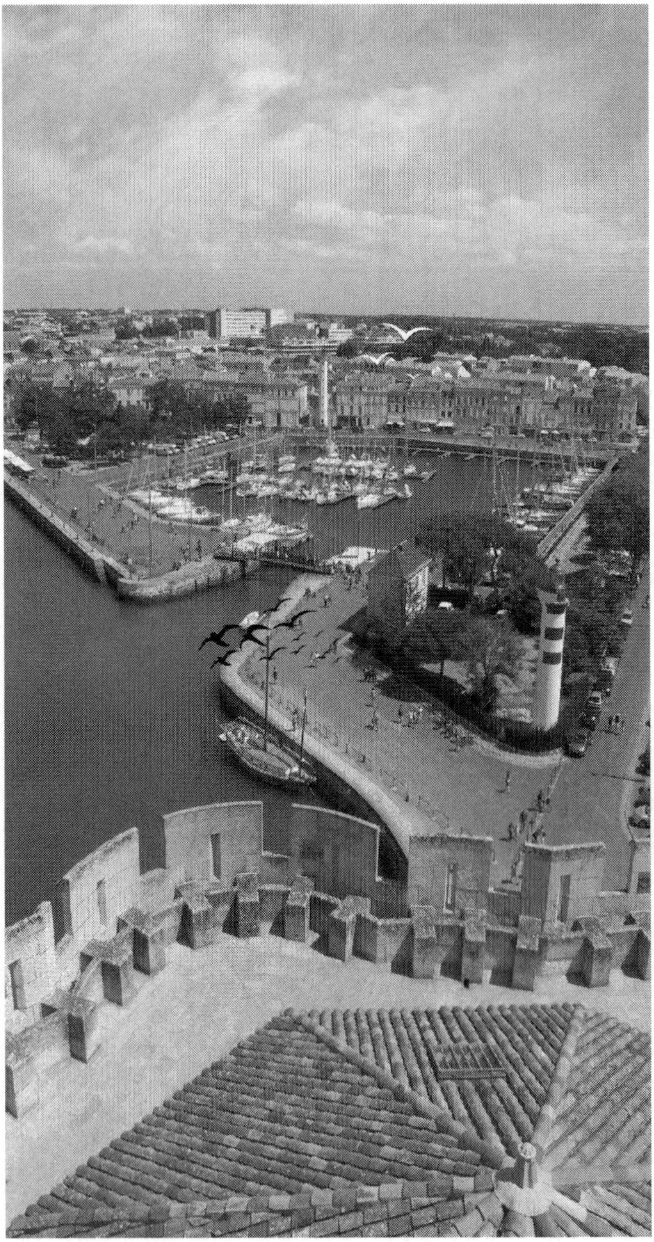

CHAPTER 9: ITINERARIES SUGGESTIONS

La Rochelle In One Day

Begin your day in the Vieux Port (Old Port), the city's beating heart, where you may marvel at the colourful boats and old architecture. While taking in the bustling environment, have a croissant and coffee at one of the riverfront cafés.

Following that, visit the gorgeous La Rochelle Aquarium, which has an incredible array of aquatic life and interactive displays, making it ideal for visitors of all ages. A short walk away, the Tour de la Chaîne and Tour Saint-Nicolas, La Rochelle's ancient towers, invite you to study their mediaeval past and enjoy panoramic views of the city from their heights.

For lunch, savour the freshest catches of the day at one of the numerous seafood eateries located near the dock. After that, wander around the city center's gorgeous streets, which are dotted with quaint stores and cafés.

Visit the Maritime Museum in the afternoon to learn about La Rochelle's rich maritime heritage. You may also take a boat excursion to nearby Île de Ré, which is noted for its beautiful beaches and charming towns.

Finish your day by visiting the lovely Parc Charruyer, a tranquil green spot ideal for rest and introspection.

Weekend Trip

Day 1:

- **Morning**: Begin your day by seeing La Rochelle's historic heart, the Old Port (Vieux Port). Stroll around the lovely coastline, admiring the colourful boats and the landmark La Rochelle Towers.
- **Lunch**: At one of the many quayside eateries, savour fresh seafood. Don't miss out on the famed mussels and oysters of the area.
- **In the afternoon**, visit the Maritime Museum (Musée Maritime), which is housed in the old Saint-Jean d'Acre tower. It sheds light on La Rochelle's maritime past.
- **Evening**: Visit the city's beautiful Aquarium, one of Europe's largest. Enjoy a fascinating aquatic adventure suitable for all ages.

Day 2:

- **In the morning,** take a short boat journey to neighbouring Île de Ré, which is known for its beautiful beaches and lovely towns. Rent a bike to enjoy the island's beautiful scenery.
- **Lunch**: In one of the island's modest restaurants, savour local delicacies like salt-marsh lamb and potato salad.
- **Afternoon**: Return to La Rochelle and learn about its fascinating history at the Towers of La Rochelle. Climb to the peak for spectacular views.
- **Evening**: Savour the flavours of classic French cuisine with a leisurely meal at one of the city's numerous gourmet restaurants.

Activities For The Whole Family With Day Trip

Day 1: Discover La Rochelle

- **Morning**: Begin your day in the famed Vieux Port (Old Port) and pay a visit to the Aquarium La Rochelle, which is a must-see for both youngsters and adults.
- **Lunch**: Sample some delectable seafood at one of the numerous eateries located around the harbour.
- **Afternoon**: Take a stroll through historic Old Town, complete with charming shops, cafés, and street entertainment. Don't miss out on the Tour de la Lanterne and Tour de la Chaîne.
- **Evening**: Dine at one of the city center's family-friendly restaurants.

Day 2: Beach Time

- **Morning**: Visit neighbouring Île de Ré, a beautiful island noted for its clean beaches. Rent bicycles and experience the natural beauty of the island.
- Pack a picnic or savour some seaside seafood for **lunch**.
- **Afternoon**: Spend the day on the island's sandy shoreline swimming, creating sandcastles or kite flying.
- **Evening**: Return to La Rochelle for a delectable meal at a local creperie or pizza.

Day 3: Historical Exploration
- **Morning**: Tour the Maritime Museum and the historic Fort Boyard, which is well-known for its television game show.
- **Lunch**: Sample classic French food at a typical brasserie.
- **Afternoon**: Visit the adjacent Château de Dampierre-sur-Boutonne, where

youngsters may journey back in time and picture themselves living in a castle.

- **Evening**: Have a leisurely meal at a delightful café.

Romantic Getaway

Day One: Arrival and Sunset Walk

When you arrive in La Rochelle, book a room at a gorgeous seaside hotel. Take a stroll around the historic Old Port and watch the sun set over the glistening seas. Dinner at a charming cafe with delicious seafood and local wines.

Day 2: Visit the Old Town

Wander through the cobblestone alleys of La Rochelle to discover its heart. For a sample of local delights, visit the beautiful Saint-Nicolas Tower, the charming La Rochelle Cathedral, and the colourful Les Halles food market.

Day 3: Island Exploration

Take a boat ride to the adjacent Île de Ré, where you'll find beautiful beaches and charming towns. Rent bicycles and enjoy the lovely scenery of the island. Dine at a beachside restaurant with ocean views.

Day 4: Unwind and Reconnect

Rekindle your romance by spending a day at the beach or relaxing at a spa. At a Michelin-starred restaurant, enjoy an intimate candlelit meal.

Day 5: Goodbye and Memories

Take one more stroll along the harbour before departing, reflecting about your fantastic La Rochelle vacation.

CHAPTER 10: USEFUL INFORMATION

Weather Condition And Best Time To Visit

Spring, from March to May, is a lovely season to visit La Rochelle. The weather begins to warm, and the city's lovely surroundings bloom with flowers. Temperatures range from 10°C to 18°C, making it a perfect time for outdoor sports and sightseeing without the throngs of summer.

Summer is the busiest season in La Rochelle, lasting from June through August. The weather is pleasant, with temperatures normally ranging from 18°C to 25°C. This is the ideal time for beachgoers and water sports enthusiasts to take advantage of the clean coastline and colourful environment. Expect greater people and higher rates throughout this season, however.

From September to November, the weather is warm and there are less tourists. The temperature ranges from 14°C to 21°C, making it an ideal time to see historical monuments, visit local markets, and sample regional cuisine.

Temperatures range from 4°C to 11°C throughout the winter months of December to February. While the weather may not be ideal for a day at the beach, La Rochelle's interior attractions, such as museums and cosy cafés, are great to explore during this slower season.

Etiquette And Customs

- **Greetings**: When entering a business, restaurant, or public venue in La Rochelle, it is usual to greet individuals with a courteous "Bonjour" (good morning) or "Bonsoir" (good evening). It is a symbol of civility and respect.

- **Dining Etiquette**: When dining in La Rochelle, keep in mind that meals are frequently seen as a leisurely event. Wait for the host to begin the meal, and keep your hands but not your elbows on the table. It is customary to say "Bon appétit" before beginning your meal.

- **Politeness**: The French value courteous gestures such as "s'il vous plaît" (please) and "merci" (thank you). When dealing with natives, being nice and patient goes a long way.

- **Language**: While many people speak English, making an effort to learn a few basic French words may be quite beneficial.

- **Dress Code**: Although La Rochelle has a relaxing beach feel, it is vital to dress smartly and follow local dress requirements when visiting religious sites.

- **Tipping** is traditional in La Rochelle, and is usually approximately 10% of the cost. However, service costs are frequently included in the bill, so double-check before giving an extra tip.

Communication And Language

The predominant language of La Rochelle is, of course, French, and it acts as a portal to the local culture. Knowing some French may enhance your experience, whether you're purchasing a café au lait at a delightful café or appreciating the nautical legacy in the Old Port.

Nonetheless, La Rochelle's history as a bustling port has left a cosmopolitan imprint. The town has a cosmopolitan flavour to it, with English,

Spanish, and Portuguese frequently heard alongside French. As you explore the town's various museums, you'll come across displays that chronicle the stories of international trade, emphasising the importance of language in this seaside treasure.

Communication in La Rochelle goes beyond words. It's in the inhabitants' warm grins, the joy of children playing by the sea, and the sounds of street musicians.

Health And Safety Recommendations

- **Sun Protection**: Because La Rochelle gets a lot of sun, remember to use sunscreen, wear a hat, and remain hydrated to avoid sunburn and dehydration.

- **Water Safety**: If you intend to swim in the Atlantic Ocean, be careful of the tides and currents. Always swim in authorised zones and obey any lifeguard cautions.
- **Pedestrian Safety:** La Rochelle is a great place to walk. Use crosswalks, follow traffic laws, and keep an eye out for bicycles while you tour the town.
- **Food and Water:** Try the local cuisine, but keep food cleanliness in mind. Stick to recognised places, and if you're concerned about tap water, drink bottled water.
- **Travel Insurance**: Make certain that you have travel insurance that covers any unexpected accidents or medical crises.
- **Local Advice:** For particular safety precautions pertaining to your visit, seek advice from locals and tourism information centres.

Currency And Money Exchange

France's official currency is the Euro (EUR). When you arrive in La Rochelle, you'll discover that using euros for most transactions is easy. currencies exchange facilities are available in banks, post offices, and even railway stations, making it simple to convert foreign currencies into euros.

It is better to utilise local banks for the best conversion rates, however ATMs are also a convenient choice. In La Rochelle, most major credit and debit cards are readily accepted, making it simple to pay for products and services. However, it's always a good idea to have some cash on hand for minor purchases or in case you come across establishments that don't accept cards.

Money-Saving Tips

- **Off-Peak Travel**: Plan your vacation for the off-season, which normally runs from late autumn to early spring. You'll save money on lodging and transport, and you'll escape the summer throngs.
- **Local Transportation**: Because La Rochelle is a walkable city, leave the vehicle at home and explore on foot. You may also hire a bike, ride a bus, or utilise the electric Yélo bikes, making mobility economical and eco-friendly.
- **food on a Budget**: Enjoy the local food without overpaying. For traditional, moderately priced lunches, look for tiny, family-run bistros, or pick up fresh food from the market and have a picnic by the harbour.
- La Rochelle has several **free attractions**, including the historic Old Port, the

coastline, and the lovely parks. It is free to walk along the city's defences or visit the different open-air markets.

- Get a **La Rochelle City Pass.** The La Rochelle City Pass includes free entrance to several of the city's best attractions as well as unrestricted public transit use.
- **Look for exclusive offers and discounts.** Many La Rochelle attractions and companies provide discounts and promotions to students, retirees, and groups. When purchasing tickets or making accommodations, be sure to inquire about discounts.
- **Accommodation**: Choose low-cost options such as hostels, guesthouses, or vacation rentals. To save money, consider sharing rooms with friends or family.
- **Booking in Advance:** Plan and book your vacation in advance. This can assist

you in obtaining better rates on flights, lodging, and activities.

Basic French Phrases

- Bonjour - "Good morning."
- S'il vous plaît - "Please"
- Oui and Non - "Yes" and "No"
- Excusez-moi - "Excuse me"
- Je suis perdu(e). - I am lost.
- Pouvez-vous me donner des directions pour... ? - Can you give me directions to...?
- Je cherche un restaurant / un bar / un hôtel. - I am looking for a restaurant / a bar / a hotel.
- Parlez-vous anglais ? - Do you speak English?
- Merci beaucoup ! - Thank you very much!

MAPS

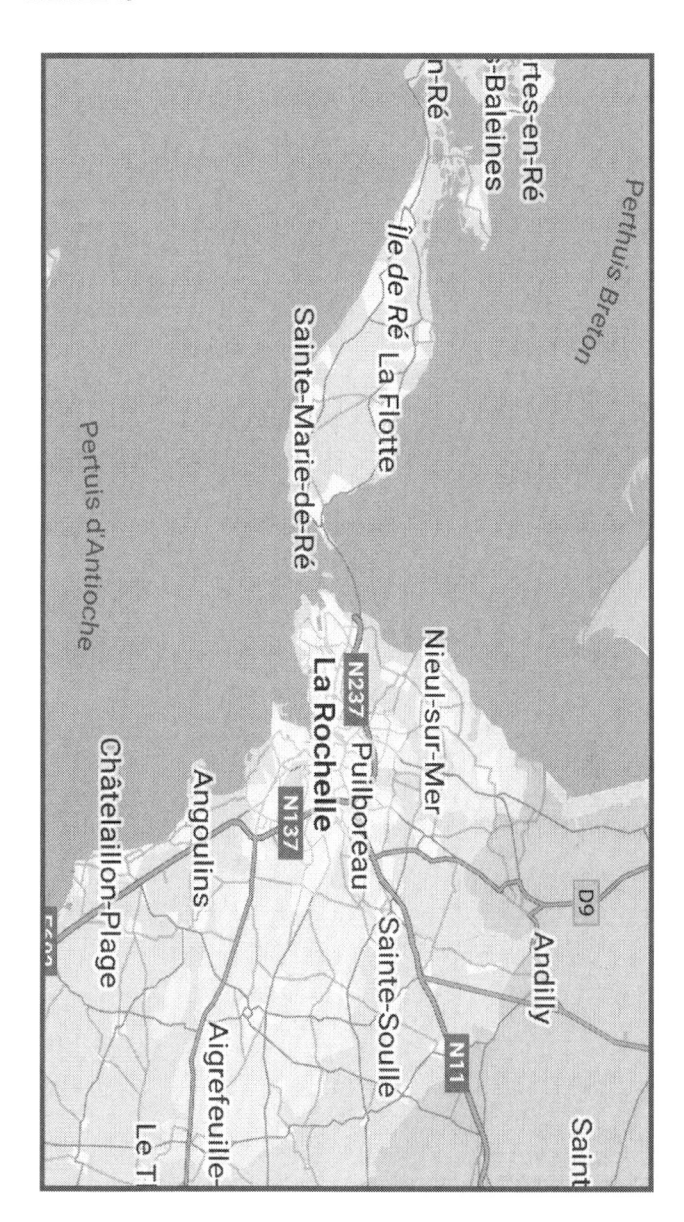

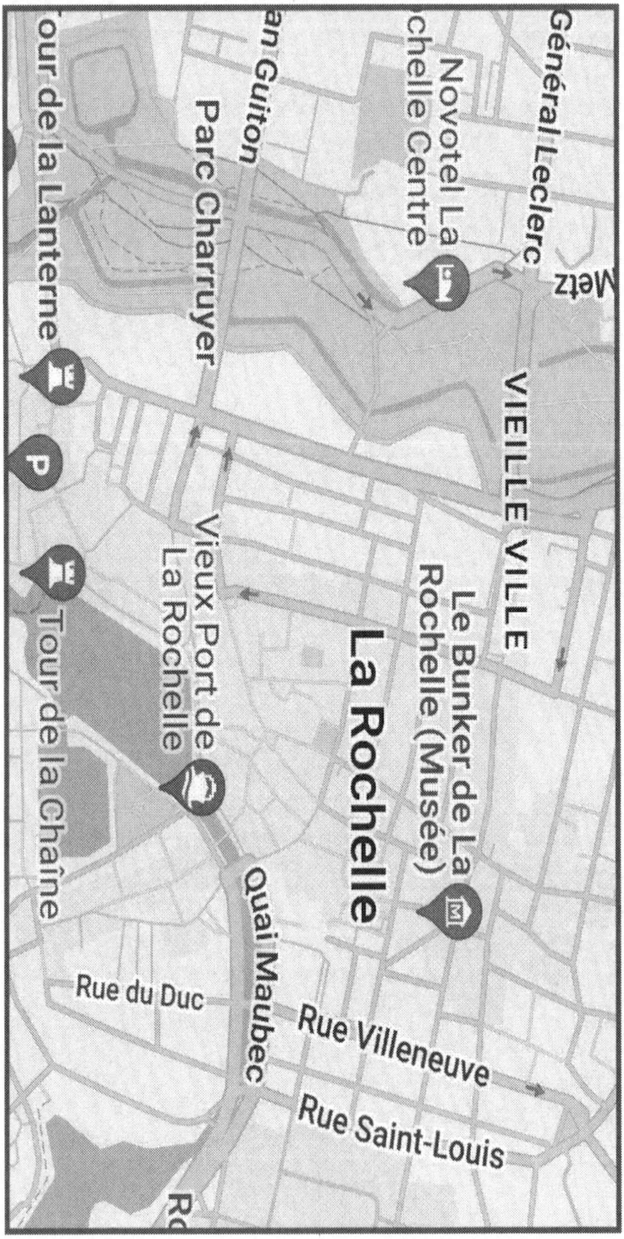
Général Leclerc
Metz
Parc Charruyer
Tour de la Lanterne
VIEILLE VILLE
Le Bunker de La Rochelle (Musée)
La Rochelle
Vieux Port de La Rochelle
Tour de la Chaîne
Quai Maubec
Rue du Duc
Rue Villeneuve
Rue Saint-Louis

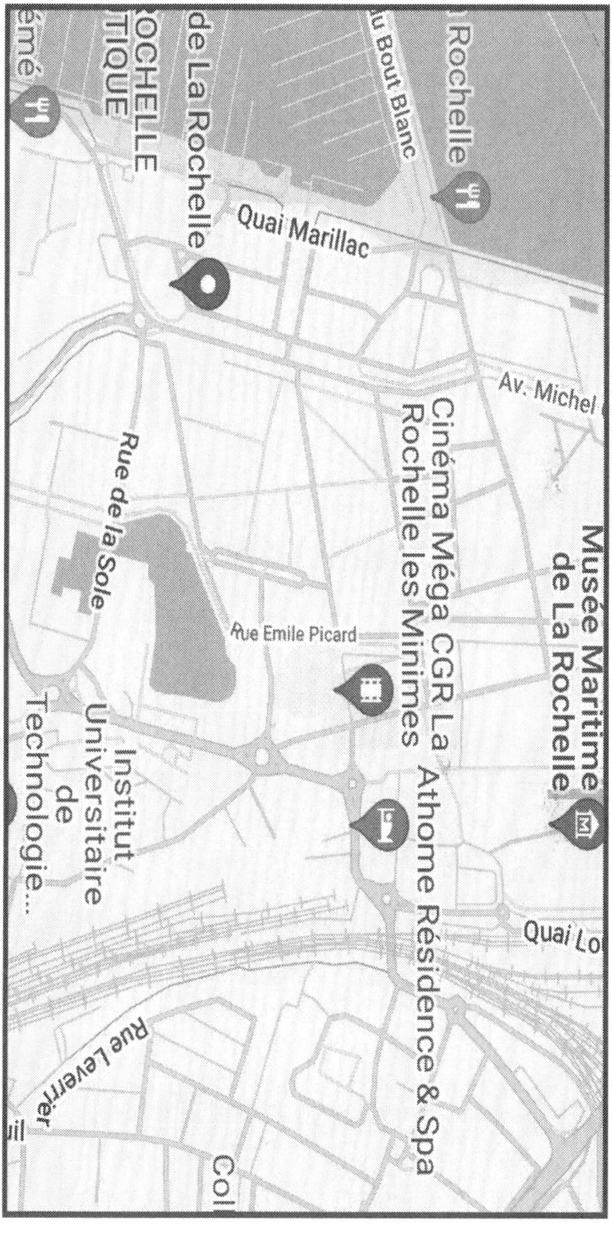
Musée Maritime de La Rochelle
Cinéma Méga CGR La Rochelle les Minimes
Athome Résidence & Spa
Quai Marillac
Av. Michel
Rue de la Sole
Rue Emile Picard
Institut Universitaire de Technologie...
Rue Leverrier
de La Rochelle

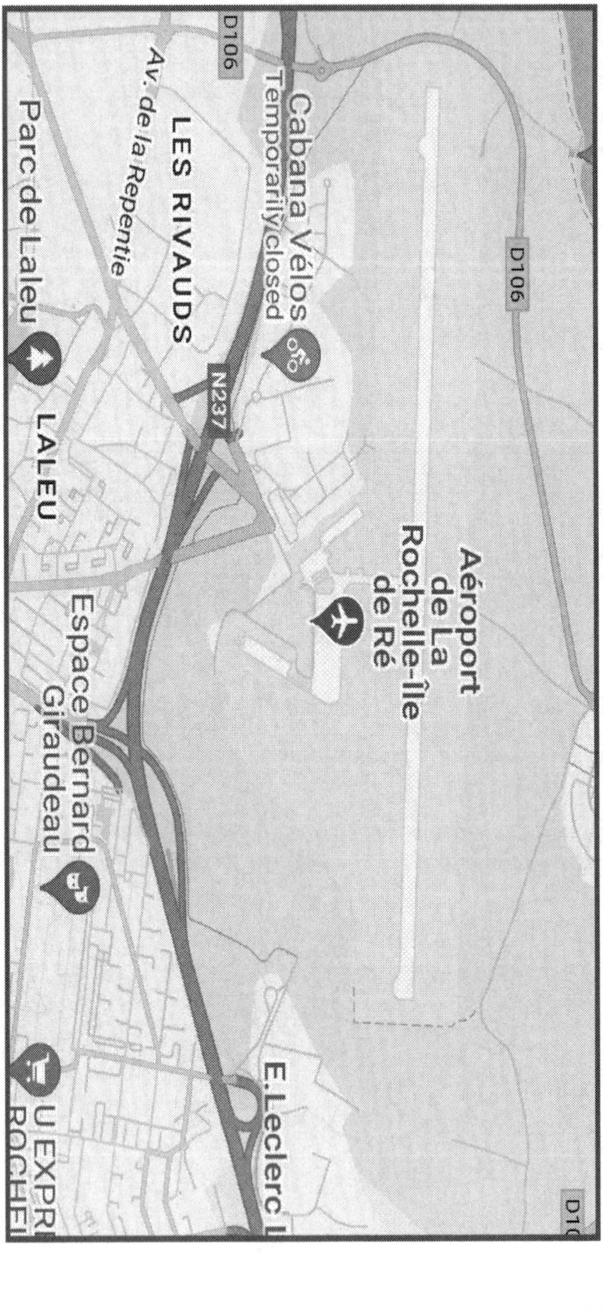
Aéroport de La Rochelle-île de Ré
Cabana Vélos
Temporarily closed
LES RIVAUDS
Av. de la Repentie
Parc de Laleu
LALEU
Espace Bernard Giraudeau
D106
N237
D106

109

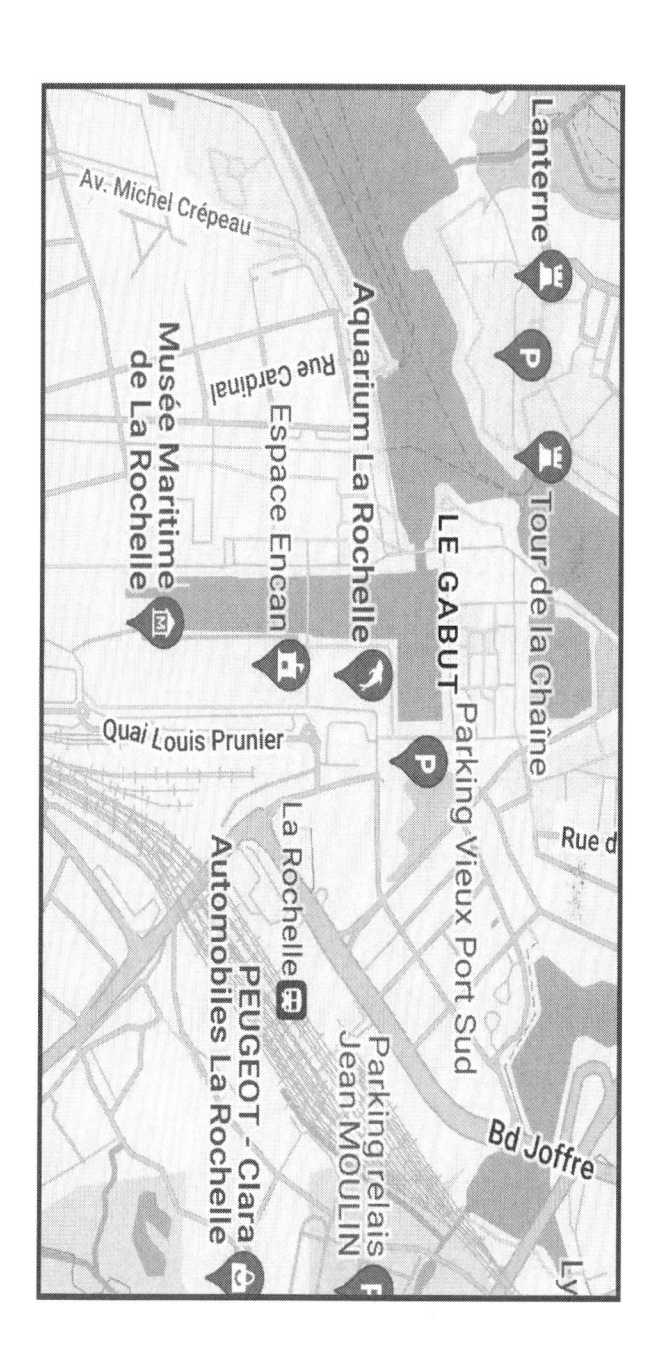

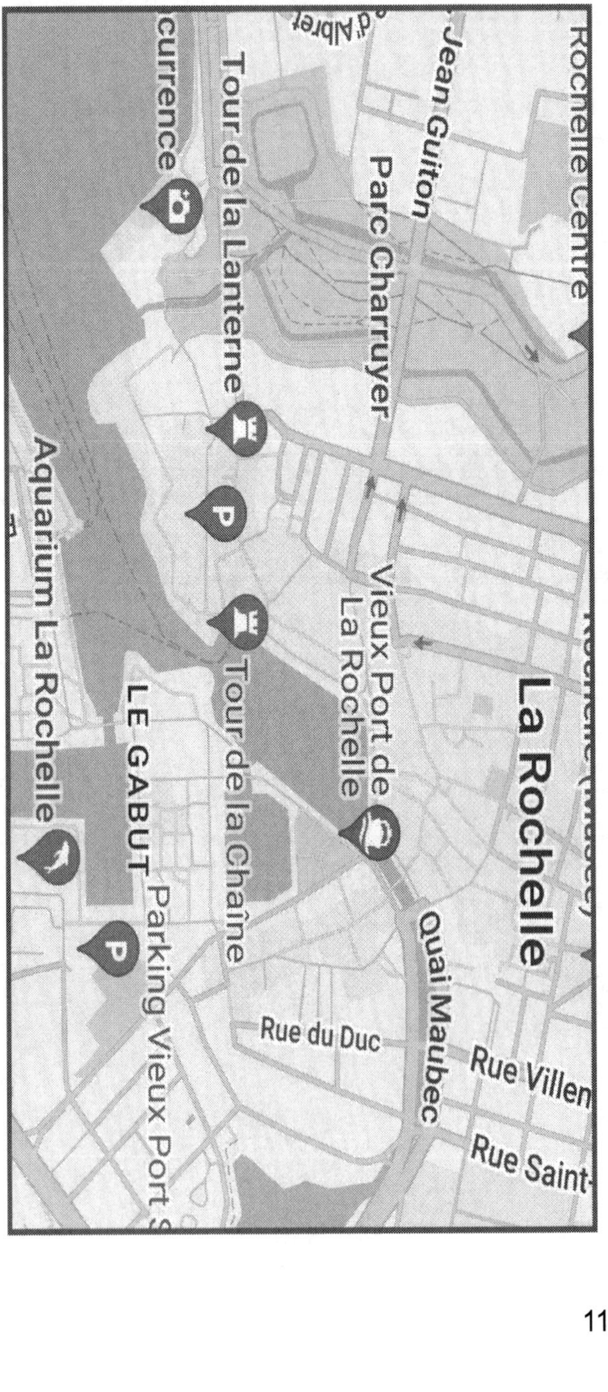
La Rochelle
Parc Charruyer
Tour de la Lanterne
Vieux Port de La Rochelle
Tour de la Chaîne
Aquarium La Rochelle
LE GABUT
Quai Maubec
Rue du Duc

Printed in Great Britain
by Amazon